BUILDING EQUITY

Proven Techniques for Growing Your Real Estate Portfolio

NELLA BYRAN

Copyright

No part of this should be reproduced without the permission of the author.

© Nella Byran 2024

Contents

Opening 4
The Power of Real Estate Equity 8
Understanding Equity 13
Strategic Property Selection 18
Leveraging Leverage 25
Equity through Renovations 31
Buy and Hold Strategies 36
Equity Crowdfunding 42
Tax Strategies for Equity Growth 48
Market Timing and Equity 54
Equity Partnerships 60
Real Estate Syndication 66
Equity Exchanges: Swapping for Strategic Growth 73
Portfolio Diversification 79
Commercial Real Estate 85
Retirement Planning with Real Estate Equity 92
Equity Preservation: Protecting Your Real Estate Wealth 99
Real Estate Exit Strategies 106
The Future of Real Estate Equity 112
Technology Integration 118
Final thought 120

Opening

In the vast landscape of investment opportunities, few vehicles offer the enduring power and potential for wealth accumulation quite like real estate. Imagine a world where your money not only works for you but also builds a sturdy foundation for future prosperity. This is the promise and allure of real estate equity.

Welcome to "Building Equity: Proven Techniques for Growing Your Real Estate Portfolio." In these pages, we embark on a journey into the heart of real estate investment, where the concept of equity reigns supreme. Equity, the magic word that represents ownership, value, and growth, is not merely a buzzword; it's the cornerstone of financial success in the real estate realm.

Throughout this book, we will delve into the myriad ways in which understanding, harnessing, and maximizing equity can transform your real estate endeavors. We'll equip you with the tools, strategies, and insights needed to navigate this dynamic landscape with confidence and foresight.

To begin, we must grasp the fundamental concept of equity and its profound impact on your portfolio's growth. As we explore the foundations of equity, you'll uncover the key principles that underpin successful real estate investment. From strategic property selection to the art of leveraging leverage, each chapter is crafted to illuminate a crucial aspect of building and expanding your real estate equity.

But this book is more than just a roadmap to financial growth; it's a guide to seizing opportunities and unlocking the full potential of your investments. We'll venture into the realm of renovations, where adding value to properties becomes a pathway to enhanced equity. We'll also explore the timeless strategy of buy and hold, a methodical approach to long-term equity accumulation that has stood the test of time.

In a rapidly evolving landscape, we cannot overlook the innovative avenues for equity growth, such as equity crowdfunding and real estate syndication. These collaborative approaches offer access to larger opportunities and the potential for exponential portfolio expansion.

Yet, our journey does not end there. We'll delve into the realm of tax strategies, market timing, and the art of portfolio diversification—all with the singular goal of maximizing your returns while mitigating risks.

As we progress, we'll uncover the nuances of commercial real estate, a realm where the potential for equity growth reaches new heights. We'll also discuss retirement planning through the lens of real estate equity, offering insights into building a secure future for yourself and your loved ones.

Throughout these pages, you'll encounter real-world examples, expert advice, and actionable steps to propel your real estate portfolio forward. Whether you're a seasoned investor seeking to optimize your equity or a newcomer eager to embark on this rewarding journey, "Building Equity" is your trusted companion.

So, join us as we navigate the terrain of real estate equity, where every decision, every acquisition, and every renovation holds the potential to shape your financial destiny. The future of real estate equity is within reach, and it's time to seize it. Welcome to a world of possibility, welcome to "Building Equity."

The Power of Real Estate Equity

Real estate equity stands as a powerful force within the realm of investments, offering a unique blend of stability, growth potential, and tangible value. It serves as the cornerstone of wealth creation for countless investors, both seasoned veterans and newcomers to the world of property ownership. Understanding the power and dynamics of real estate equity is not merely advantageous—it's essential for anyone looking to build a robust and sustainable financial future.

What is Real Estate Equity?

At its core, real estate equity represents ownership. It's the portion of the property that you truly own outright, free from any debts or liabilities against it. When you purchase a property, whether it's a residential home, a commercial building, or a piece of land, your equity in that property is the difference between its market value and the outstanding balance on any loans or mortgages.

For example, if you buy a home for $300,000 and take out a mortgage for $250,000, your initial equity is $50,000. As you pay down the mortgage over time, and/or as the property appreciates in value, your equity grows. This growth is where the power of real estate equity truly shines.

Stability and Wealth Preservation

One of the primary attractions of real estate equity is its stability. Unlike other forms of investments that can be subject to volatile market swings, real estate has historically shown a propensity for steady, long-term growth. Properties tend to appreciate over time, often outpacing inflation rates, which means your equity grows simply by owning the property.

Additionally, real estate equity serves as a form of forced savings. When you make mortgage payments, a portion of that payment goes towards reducing the loan balance (the principal), thus increasing your equity. This process builds over time, leading to a situation where you not only own an appreciating asset but also steadily increase the amount you truly own within that asset.

Leverage and Multiplying Your Investment

Another powerful aspect of real estate equity is leverage. Real estate is one of the few investments where you can use borrowed funds (a mortgage) to acquire an asset. When you put down a portion of the property's value as a down payment, you control the entire property and benefit from its appreciation, even though you only invested a fraction of the total value.

For instance, if you purchase a $200,000 property with a $40,000 down payment and the property appreciates by 5%, your actual return on investment is much higher than 5% because you're earning on the entire $200,000, not just your $40,000 investment. This amplification of returns through leverage is a key factor in the power of real estate equity.

Building Wealth and Passive Income

Real estate equity is not just about the value of your property increasing; it's also about the potential for generating passive income. Rental properties, for example, can provide a steady stream of income that builds on top of the equity growth. As you pay down the mortgage (building equity) and collect rental payments, your net worth increases, and you establish a source of passive income that can support your financial goals.

Accessing Capital and Financial Flexibility

Equity in real estate also offers a unique advantage when it comes to accessing capital. If you've built up substantial equity in a property, you can leverage that equity to obtain loans or lines of credit. This capital can be used for various purposes, such as funding new investments, renovating existing properties to increase their value, or even as a source of emergency funds.

Tax Advantages

Real estate equity comes with a host of tax advantages as well. Interest on mortgages, property taxes, and certain expenses related to property ownership can often be deducted from your taxable income. Additionally, when you sell a property, there are opportunities to defer or minimize capital gains taxes through strategies like 1031 exchanges.

In conclusion, the power of real estate equity lies in its multifaceted nature. It's a stable and appreciating asset that offers leverage, passive income, access to capital, tax advantages, and the potential for long-term wealth creation. Whether you're a seasoned investor looking to expand your portfolio or someone just starting on their investment journey, understanding and harnessing the power of real estate equity can be a transformative step towards financial independence and security.

Understanding Equity

Understanding equity in the context of real estate is fundamental to building a successful and growing portfolio. It forms the bedrock upon which your investments stand, influencing every decision from property selection to financing strategies. Let's delve into the essence of equity and its role as the cornerstone for portfolio growth.

Equity in real estate is essentially ownership. When you own a property, your equity is the difference between its market value and any outstanding debts or liabilities against it. It's the portion of the property that truly belongs to you, free and clear. This concept is vital because it determines the true value of your investment and serves as a measure of your financial stake in the property.

Equity as a Measure of Wealth

Think of equity as a measure of wealth accumulation within your real estate holdings. As you pay down the mortgage on a property or as the property appreciates in value, your equity grows. This growth represents the tangible increase in your net worth tied to that property. The more equity you have in a property, the more wealth you've built within that asset.

Equity and Market Value

Understanding equity also involves recognizing its relationship with market value. Market value is the current worth of your property in the open market, while equity is your stake in that value. When market values rise, your equity naturally increases, often providing a significant boost to your overall portfolio's value. Conversely, during market downturns, your equity can be impacted if property values decline.

Building Equity Through Principal Payments

One of the primary ways to build equity is through principal payments on your mortgage. Each mortgage payment you make includes a portion that goes towards reducing the loan balance (the principal) and another portion for interest. Over time, as you make these payments, the principal decreases, and your equity increases. This process is often referred to as "amortization," where the loan is paid off gradually, increasing your ownership stake with each payment.

Equity and Appreciation

Property appreciation is another key driver of equity growth. When a property's value increases over time due to factors such as market demand, renovations, or improvements in the neighborhood, your equity grows along with it. Appreciation can be a powerful wealth-building tool, especially in markets where property values tend to rise steadily.

Using Equity for Further Investments

Equity in one property can also be leveraged to acquire additional properties or investments. For example, if you've built up substantial equity in a property, you can refinance or take out a home equity loan to access that equity in the form of cash. This cash can then be used for down payments on new properties, funding renovations, or other investment opportunities. This strategy allows you to amplify your portfolio growth by using existing equity to acquire more assets.

The Role of Equity in Risk Management

Equity also plays a crucial role in risk management within your portfolio. Properties with higher levels of equity are more resilient to market fluctuations and economic downturns. If property values decrease, having a significant equity cushion provides a buffer against potential losses. It also reduces the risk of being "underwater" on a mortgage, where you owe more than the property is worth.

In conclusion, understanding equity is essential for anyone looking to build a successful real estate portfolio. It forms the foundation upon which wealth is built, representing your ownership stake in properties. Whether through principal payments, property appreciation, or leveraging existing equity for further investments, the growth of equity drives portfolio expansion and wealth accumulation. By mastering the fundamentals of equity, you can make informed decisions, manage risks effectively, and pave the way for long-term financial success in the world of real estate investing.

Strategic Property Selection

Strategic property selection is a cornerstone of success in real estate investing. It's not merely about finding any property; it's about finding the right property that aligns with your investment goals, risk tolerance, and financial strategy. This process involves careful analysis, research, and consideration of various factors to ensure that the properties you choose are the building blocks for a successful portfolio. Let's delve into the detailed aspects of strategic property selection:

Market Research and Analysis

The first step in strategic property selection is thorough market research and analysis. This involves studying local real estate markets to understand trends, supply and demand dynamics, property values, rental rates (if applicable), and economic indicators. By identifying markets with strong growth potential, you can narrow down your focus to areas where investing is likely to yield favorable returns.

Investment Goals and Strategy Alignment

Before selecting a property, it's crucial to define your investment goals and strategy. Are you looking for long-term appreciation, rental income, or a combination of both? Your goals will influence the type of properties you target. For example, if you're seeking steady rental income, you might focus on multi-family units or properties in areas with high rental demand. If you're aiming for appreciation, you might look for emerging neighborhoods with growth potential.

Property Criteria

Once you've identified your market and investment goals, it's time to define your property criteria. This includes factors such as:

Property Type: Will you invest in single-family homes, multi-family units, commercial properties, or vacant land? Each type has its advantages and considerations.

Location: The old adage "location, location, location" holds true. Consider factors such as proximity to amenities (schools, shopping, transportation), neighborhood quality, safety, and future development plans.

Condition: Are you looking for turnkey properties, or are you open to properties that need renovations or repairs? The condition of the property will affect your upfront costs and potential returns.

Price Range: Define your budget and target price range. This will help narrow down your search and ensure you're focusing on properties within your financial means.

Return on Investment (ROI) Analysis

A crucial aspect of strategic property selection is conducting a thorough ROI analysis. This involves calculating potential returns and expenses associated with the property. Considerations include:

Rental Income: If you're investing in rental properties, estimate the potential rental income based on market rates and occupancy rates.

Operating Expenses: Factor in expenses such as property taxes, insurance, maintenance, property management fees (if applicable), utilities, and any homeowner association (HOA) fees.

Cash Flow: Calculate the net cash flow by subtracting expenses from rental income. Positive cash flow is ideal, indicating that the property generates more income than it costs to operate.

Cap Rate and Cash-on-Cash Return: These metrics help evaluate the property's potential return on investment. The cap rate compares the property's net operating income to its purchase price, while cash-on-cash return considers the cash invested compared to the annual cash flow.

Risk Assessment

Every investment carries inherent risks, and strategic property selection involves assessing and mitigating these risks. Consider factors such as:

Market Stability: Is the local market stable, or is it prone to fluctuations? Stable markets offer predictability and lower risk.

Economic Factors: Consider economic indicators such as job growth, population trends, and industry diversification. A strong economy generally supports real estate appreciation and rental demand.

Property-Specific Risks: Evaluate property-specific risks such as potential maintenance issues, vacancy rates, tenant turnover, and regulatory changes.

Due Diligence and Property Inspection

Before finalizing a property purchase, thorough due diligence is essential. This includes:

Property Inspection: Hire a professional inspector to assess the property's condition. Identify any hidden issues that could affect its value or require costly repairs.

Title Search: Ensure there are no liens, encumbrances, or legal issues with the property's title.

Financial Analysis: Verify the property's financials, including rent rolls (for rental properties), operating expenses, and historical performance.

Long-Term Vision

Strategic property selection is not just about the immediate gains but also about the long-term vision for your portfolio. Consider how each property fits into your overall investment strategy. Will it complement existing properties? Does it align with your portfolio diversification goals? Having a clear vision for how each property contributes to your portfolio's growth and stability is key.

In conclusion, strategic property selection forms the building blocks for a successful real estate portfolio. It involves thorough market research, alignment with investment goals, defining property criteria, conducting ROI analysis, assessing risks, due diligence, and maintaining a long-term vision. By meticulously evaluating properties based on these criteria, investors can identify opportunities with the potential for growth, rental income, and long-term appreciation. Strategic property selection is not just about finding properties—it's about finding the right properties that lay the foundation for a prosperous and diversified real estate portfolio.

Leveraging Leverage

Leveraging leverage in real estate is a powerful strategy that allows investors to amplify their equity growth and expand their portfolios using borrowed funds. When used wisely, financing can be a potent tool for maximizing returns and accelerating wealth accumulation. Let's explore the detailed aspects of leveraging leverage in real estate:

The Concept of Leverage

Leverage, in the context of real estate, refers to using borrowed funds (such as mortgages or loans) to acquire an investment property. Instead of paying the full purchase price upfront with cash, investors contribute a portion of the property's value as a down payment and finance the rest. This means that with a relatively small amount of your own money, you control a much larger asset.

Amplifying Returns

One of the primary benefits of leveraging leverage is the ability to amplify returns. Let's illustrate this with an example:

Suppose you purchase a $200,000 property with a 20% down payment ($40,000) and finance the remaining $160,000 with a mortgage. If the property appreciates by 5% in a year, the actual return on your investment is not just 5% on your $40,000 down payment but 25% on the entire $200,000 property value ($10,000 increase on a $40,000 investment).

This amplification of returns allows investors to achieve higher percentage returns on their invested capital compared to purchasing properties outright with cash.

Using Leverage for Portfolio Expansion

Leveraging leverage also enables investors to expand their portfolios more rapidly. Since you're not tying up all your capital in a single property, you can use the same funds to acquire multiple properties. For example, instead of buying one $200,000 property with cash, you could potentially purchase five $200,000 properties with 20% down payments on each, greatly diversifying your holdings.

Cash Flow Considerations

While leveraging leverage can be highly beneficial for equity growth and portfolio expansion, it's important to consider cash flow. Mortgage payments, interest, property taxes, insurance, and maintenance costs are ongoing expenses that must be factored into the equation. Investors need to ensure that rental income or other sources of revenue from the property cover these expenses and ideally generate positive cash flow.

Risk Management

As with any investment strategy, leveraging leverage comes with risks that need to be managed. One significant risk is the potential for negative equity if property values decline. If the property's value drops below the outstanding loan balance, you could be "underwater," owing more than the property is worth. This situation can limit your options if you need to sell the property.

Additionally, interest rates play a crucial role in the cost of leveraging. If interest rates rise significantly, it can increase the cost of borrowing and impact cash flow. Investors should consider fixed-rate mortgages or other strategies to mitigate interest rate risk.

Qualifying for Financing

To leverage leverage effectively, investors need to qualify for financing from lenders. This involves demonstrating a strong credit history, sufficient income to cover mortgage payments, a low debt-to-income ratio, and a favorable debt-service coverage ratio (for rental properties). Lenders will also consider the property's appraised value and potential rental income.

Using Equity Build-Up

Another benefit of leveraging leverage is the equity build-up over time. As you make mortgage payments, a portion goes towards reducing the loan balance (the principal), increasing your equity. This process of equity build-up is essentially a form of forced savings, where you're gradually building wealth through property ownership.

In conclusion, leveraging leverage through financing is a potent strategy for maximizing equity growth and portfolio expansion in real estate. By using borrowed funds to acquire properties, investors can amplify their returns, diversify their holdings, and benefit from the potential for long-term appreciation. However, it's crucial to carefully manage cash flow, consider risks such as negative equity, and ensure that financing terms are favorable. When used wisely and with a clear understanding of the risks and rewards, leveraging leverage can be a valuable tool for building a robust and prosperous real estate portfolio.

Equity through Renovations

Equity through renovations is a strategic approach that allows real estate investors to enhance the value of their properties, thereby increasing their equity. This process involves making improvements, upgrades, and renovations to a property with the goal of maximizing its market value. Let's explore how renovations can serve as a pathway to significant equity growth:

Renovations are a direct way to increase the appeal and value of a property. This can be achieved through both cosmetic upgrades and functional improvements. Cosmetic upgrades may include fresh paint, updated fixtures, modernizing the kitchen or bathrooms, and enhancing curb appeal with landscaping. These enhancements not only make the property more visually appealing to potential buyers or renters but also contribute to its overall market value.

Functional improvements, on the other hand, focus on enhancing the property's functionality, efficiency, and comfort. This may involve upgrading HVAC systems, replacing old plumbing or electrical systems, installing energy-efficient appliances, or improving the layout to maximize space utilization. By addressing these aspects, renovations not only make the property more attractive but also increase its desirability and market value.

One of the key benefits of equity through renovations is the potential for a significant return on investment (ROI). When done strategically, renovations can result in a higher selling price or rental income, far exceeding the cost of the renovations themselves. For example, investing $20,000 in kitchen upgrades could potentially increase the property's value by $30,000 or more, leading to a substantial ROI.

Renovations also allow investors to differentiate their properties in a competitive market. By adding unique features or modern amenities, a property can stand out among similar listings, attracting more interest from potential buyers or tenants. This increased demand can lead to faster sales or higher rental rates, further boosting equity.

Moreover, renovations can extend the lifespan of a property and reduce maintenance costs in the long run. Upgrading to durable materials or energy-efficient systems not only adds value but also lowers ongoing expenses, such as utility bills and repair costs. This improved efficiency and reduced maintenance burden contribute to the property's overall value and appeal.

It's important to note that the extent and type of renovations should align with the property's market and target demographic. Understanding the preferences and expectations of potential buyers or renters is crucial in determining which renovations will yield the highest returns. For example, investing in luxury finishes in a mid-range neighborhood may not result in a significant increase in value.

Timing is also a critical factor in equity through renovations. Choosing the right time to renovate, such as during periods of low market activity or before listing a property for sale, can maximize the impact of the improvements. Renovations done strategically before selling can often result in a higher sale price and a quicker sale, allowing investors to capitalize on their equity growth sooner.

In conclusion, equity through renovations offers real estate investors a powerful strategy for increasing the value of their properties and growing their equity. By making targeted improvements that enhance both the visual appeal and functionality of a property, investors can command higher selling prices, attract quality tenants, and achieve a significant ROI. However, it's essential to carefully plan and execute renovations, considering market trends, target demographics, and timing to ensure optimal results. When done effectively, renovations can be a key driver of equity growth and overall portfolio success in the dynamic world of real estate investing.

Buy and Hold Strategies

Buy and hold strategies represent a timeless approach to real estate investing focused on long-term equity accumulation. This strategy involves acquiring properties with the intention of holding onto them for an extended period, often years or even decades. The goal is to benefit from appreciation, rental income, and the gradual build-up of equity over time. Let's delve into the details of buy and hold strategies and how they contribute to long-term equity accumulation:

The Foundation of Buy and Hold

At the heart of the buy and hold strategy is the belief in the long-term growth potential of real estate. Investors who adopt this approach seek to capitalize on the historical trend of real estate values appreciating over time. Rather than aiming for quick profits through flips or short-term investments, buy and hold investors prioritize stability, cash flow, and the steady growth of their equity positions.

Benefits of Buy and Hold

Appreciation: One of the primary benefits of buy and hold investing is property appreciation. Over time, properties tend to increase in value due to factors such as inflation, market demand, and improvements in the surrounding area. By holding onto a property for an extended period, investors can benefit from this appreciation, which contributes to the growth of equity.

Rental Income: Buy and hold properties often generate rental income, especially in markets with strong demand for housing. This steady stream of rental income provides a reliable source of cash flow, which can be used to cover mortgage payments, property expenses, and even contribute to additional investments. The combination of rental income and property appreciation enhances the overall return on investment.

Equity Build-Up: As mortgage payments are made over time, the loan balance (the principal) decreases, while the property value typically increases. This process of equity build-up occurs gradually but steadily, contributing to the investor's ownership stake in the property. With each payment, investors are building equity and increasing their net worth.

Tax Benefits: Buy and hold investors also benefit from various tax advantages associated with real estate ownership. Mortgage interest, property taxes, depreciation, and certain expenses can often be deducted from taxable income, reducing the investor's tax burden. Additionally, long-term capital gains tax rates are typically lower than short-term rates, incentivizing investors to hold onto properties for extended periods.

Keys to Success

Patience and Long-Term Vision: Buy and hold investing requires patience and a long-term vision.

Investors must be willing to ride out market fluctuations and economic cycles, trusting in the historical trend of real estate values appreciating over time. By maintaining a long-term perspective, investors can avoid making impulsive decisions based on short-term market conditions.

Property Selection: Choosing the right properties is crucial for buy and hold success. Investors should focus on properties in desirable locations with strong growth potential. Factors such as neighborhood quality, proximity to amenities, school districts, and future development plans should all be considered. Additionally, properties with the potential for value-add opportunities through renovations or improvements can further enhance equity growth.

Cash Flow Management: Managing cash flow is essential for buy and hold investors, especially when properties are generating rental income. Investors should ensure that rental income covers mortgage payments, property taxes, insurance, maintenance costs, and vacancy factors. Positive cash flow not only ensures the property is self-sustaining but also provides additional funds for reinvestment or reserves.

Regular Maintenance and Upkeep: To preserve and enhance property value, regular maintenance and upkeep are necessary. This includes addressing repairs promptly, conducting routine inspections, and investing in property improvements over time. Well-maintained properties not only attract quality tenants but also tend to appreciate more in value.

In conclusion, buy and hold strategies represent a proven method for long-term equity accumulation in real estate. By acquiring properties with the intention of holding onto them for extended periods, investors can benefit from appreciation, rental income, equity build-up, and tax advantages. Success in buy and hold investing requires patience, careful property selection, effective cash flow management, and ongoing property maintenance. When executed with a long-term vision, buy and hold strategies can serve as a reliable pathway to building substantial equity and wealth through real estate.

Equity Crowdfunding

Equity crowdfunding has emerged as an innovative and collaborative approach to real estate investing, allowing individuals to pool their resources and participate in projects that were once out of reach for individual investors. This method democratizes real estate investing, opening up opportunities for portfolio expansion and diversification. Let's explore the details of equity crowdfunding and how it enables collaborative investing for the growth of real estate portfolios:

Equity crowdfunding in real estate involves a group of investors collectively funding a real estate project through an online platform. Instead of a single investor or institution providing the entire capital, multiple investors contribute smaller amounts to finance the project. Each investor receives ownership shares or equity in the property, proportional to their investment.

Accessibility and Diversification

One of the primary benefits of equity crowdfunding is its accessibility. It allows individual investors to participate in high-quality real estate projects with relatively low minimum investment amounts. This opens up opportunities for investors who may not have the capital to purchase entire properties on their own. By pooling funds with others, investors can access a diversified range of properties across different locations and asset classes.

Reduced Barriers to Entry

Equity crowdfunding removes many of the traditional barriers to entry in real estate investing. Investors do not need extensive industry knowledge, connections, or large amounts of capital to participate. The online platforms facilitate the entire process, from property selection and due diligence to investment management and distributions. This ease of access allows a broader range of investors to build and expand their real estate portfolios.

Portfolio Expansion and Risk Mitigation

Collaborative investing through equity crowdfunding enables investors to diversify their portfolios more easily. Instead of investing in a single property, investors can spread their funds across multiple properties or projects. This diversification helps mitigate risks by reducing exposure to the performance of a single asset. If one property underperforms, the impact on the overall portfolio is minimized.

Transparency and Due Diligence

Equity crowdfunding platforms provide transparency and access to detailed information about each investment opportunity. Investors can review property details, financial projections, market analysis, and the track record of the project sponsors or developers. This transparency allows investors to conduct thorough due diligence and make informed investment decisions.

Passive Income and Capital Appreciation

Investing in real estate through equity crowdfunding offers the potential for both passive income and capital appreciation. Investors may receive regular distributions from rental income generated by the property. Additionally, as the property appreciates in value over time, investors benefit from the increase in equity. These dual sources of return provide a balanced approach to wealth accumulation.

Professional Management and Expertise

Equity crowdfunding platforms often partner with experienced real estate professionals and property managers. This allows investors to benefit from the expertise of industry experts who handle property operations, tenant management, maintenance, and other aspects of real estate investment. Investors can leverage the knowledge and skills of these professionals without the need for direct involvement in property management.

Exit Opportunities

Equity crowdfunding investments typically have a defined investment horizon, after which investors can expect an exit strategy. This may include selling the property, refinancing, or distributing proceeds to investors. Having a clear exit plan allows investors to realize their gains and potentially reinvest in new opportunities, further expanding their portfolios.

Regulatory Considerations

It's important to note that equity crowdfunding in real estate is subject to regulations to protect investors. Platforms must comply with securities laws and regulations, and investments are typically open to accredited investors or conducted under Regulation A+ offerings. These regulations aim to ensure transparency, investor protection, and compliance with financial reporting standards.

In conclusion, equity crowdfunding offers a collaborative and accessible approach to real estate investing, allowing investors to pool their resources for portfolio expansion and diversification. Through online platforms, individuals can participate in high-quality real estate projects with lower barriers to entry, benefiting from passive income, capital appreciation, and professional management. The transparency, due diligence, and defined exit strategies provided by equity crowdfunding platforms contribute to a more informed and secure investment experience. By harnessing the power of collaborative investing, investors can build wealth, access new opportunities, and navigate the real estate market with confidence.

Tax Strategies for Equity Growth

Tax strategies play a crucial role in real estate investing, allowing investors to maximize returns and optimize their equity growth. Understanding and leveraging tax benefits can significantly enhance the profitability of real estate investments. Let's delve into the details of tax strategies for equity growth in real estate:

Depreciation Deductions

Depreciation is a valuable tax benefit available to real estate investors. The IRS allows investors to deduct a portion of the property's value as a depreciation expense each year, even though the property may actually be appreciating in value. This non-cash deduction helps offset rental income and reduces taxable income, thereby lowering the investor's tax liability. Depreciation can be a powerful tool for increasing cash flow and maximizing returns, especially for rental properties.

1031 Exchanges

A 1031 exchange, also known as a like-kind exchange, is a tax-deferred strategy that allows investors to sell a property and reinvest the proceeds into a similar property without paying capital gains taxes at the time of the sale. This enables investors to defer taxes on the capital gains, providing more capital for reinvestment and equity growth. By continually exchanging properties through 1031 exchanges, investors can defer capital gains taxes indefinitely, allowing their equity to grow uninterrupted.

Capital Gains Treatment

When a property is sold for a profit, the gain is typically subject to capital gains taxes. However, long-term capital gains tax rates are generally lower than ordinary income tax rates. Real estate investors can benefit from this preferential treatment by holding onto properties for more than one year before selling. This allows them to qualify for long-term capital gains tax rates, which can result in significant tax savings and higher after-tax returns.

Passive Activity Losses

Real estate investments often generate passive income, such as rental income, and passive losses, such as expenses exceeding income. The IRS allows investors to offset passive losses against passive income, reducing the overall tax liability. This means that losses from one rental property can be used to offset gains from another, optimizing tax efficiency. Additionally, unused passive losses can be carried forward to future years, providing a valuable tax deduction in subsequent years.

Cost Segregation

Cost segregation is a tax planning strategy that involves breaking down the components of a property's value into shorter-lived assets for depreciation purposes. This allows investors to accelerate depreciation deductions on certain components, such as fixtures, appliances, and improvements, which typically have shorter useful lives than the building itself. By front-loading depreciation deductions, investors can reduce taxable income in the early years of ownership, providing more cash flow for reinvestment and equity growth.

Real Estate Professional Status

Investors who qualify as real estate professionals under IRS rules can benefit from special tax treatment. Real estate professionals are not subject to passive activity loss limitations, allowing them to deduct all real estate losses against other income, such as wages or business income. This can result in substantial tax savings and a more efficient use of deductions to maximize equity growth.

Utilizing Opportunity Zones

Opportunity Zones are designated areas where investors can receive tax incentives for investing in economically distressed communities. By investing capital gains in Opportunity Zone Funds, investors can defer and potentially reduce capital gains taxes. If the investment is held for a certain period, additional tax benefits, such as partial or complete exclusion of capital gains, may apply. This strategy not only supports community development but also provides tax advantages for equity growth.

Mortgage Interest Deduction

Real estate investors can deduct mortgage interest on loans used to acquire, improve, or refinance investment properties. This deduction applies to both primary and secondary residences, as well as investment properties. By deducting mortgage interest, investors reduce their taxable income, resulting in lower taxes and higher after-tax returns. This tax benefit can significantly enhance cash flow and equity growth, especially for properties with substantial mortgage debt.

In conclusion, tax strategies are essential tools for real estate investors seeking to maximize equity growth and returns. By leveraging depreciation deductions, 1031 exchanges, capital gains treatment, passive activity losses, cost segregation, real estate professional status, Opportunity Zones, mortgage interest deductions, and other tax benefits, investors can optimize their tax liabilities and increase their after-tax profits. These strategies provide a means to preserve and enhance equity, reduce taxable income, and free up capital for further investments. Understanding and implementing effective tax strategies are key components of a successful real estate investment plan, allowing investors to build wealth and achieve long-term financial goals through real estate.

Market Timing and Equity

Market timing plays a significant role in real estate investing, as it can have a substantial impact on equity growth. Investors who are able to capitalize on market cycles—recognizing when to buy, hold, or sell properties based on market conditions—stand to maximize their returns and build substantial equity. Let's explore the relationship between market timing and equity growth in real estate:

Understanding Market Cycles

Real estate markets go through cycles of expansion, peak, contraction, and trough. These cycles are influenced by various factors such as economic conditions, interest rates, housing supply and demand, and local market dynamics. Understanding these cycles is essential for investors to make informed decisions about when to enter, exit, or hold onto properties.

Buying in a Buyer's Market

A buyer's market occurs when there is an abundance of properties for sale, leading to lower prices and increased negotiating power for buyers. Investors looking to capitalize on equity growth may find opportunities to acquire properties at below-market prices during a buyer's market. Buying low allows investors to benefit from potential appreciation when the market rebounds.

Holding During Stability

During periods of market stability, where supply and demand are balanced, holding onto properties can be advantageous for equity growth. Rental income remains steady, and property values typically appreciate at a moderate pace. Investors who hold onto properties during stable market conditions can benefit from long-term equity growth and cash flow.

Selling at the Peak

Recognizing the peak of a market cycle is crucial for investors looking to capitalize on maximum equity growth. The peak is characterized by high demand, rising prices, and increased competition among buyers. Investors may consider selling properties at or near the peak to realize substantial gains in equity. This strategy allows them to lock in profits before a potential market downturn.

Timing the Market Downturn

Market downturns, also known as buyer's markets, present unique opportunities for savvy investors. During these periods, property values may decline, creating opportunities to acquire properties at discounted prices. Investors with available capital can capitalize on market downturns by purchasing undervalued properties. As the market eventually recovers, these properties can appreciate in value, leading to significant equity growth.

Strategic Portfolio Adjustments

Market timing also involves strategic portfolio adjustments based on changing market conditions. For example, investors may consider selling underperforming properties or properties in markets expected to decline in value. They can then reinvest the proceeds into properties with higher growth potential or in emerging markets. By actively managing their portfolios, investors can optimize equity growth and minimize risks.

Long-Term Investment Horizon

While market timing is important, it's essential for investors to maintain a long-term investment horizon. Real estate markets can be cyclical, and attempting to time the market perfectly can be challenging. Investors who focus on the fundamental value of properties, cash flow, and economic indicators can achieve sustained equity growth over the long term. Patience and a disciplined approach to investing are key factors in successful market timing strategies.

Consideration of Local Market Factors

Local market factors can greatly influence market timing decisions. Real estate is inherently local, and market conditions can vary widely from one region to another. Factors such as job growth, population trends, infrastructure development, and housing supply can impact market cycles. Investors should conduct thorough research and analysis of their target markets to make informed decisions based on local conditions.

In conclusion, market timing plays a crucial role in maximizing equity growth in real estate investing. By recognizing and capitalizing on market cycles—buying in buyer's markets, holding during stability, selling at the peak, and timing market downturns—investors can optimize their returns and build substantial equity over time. However, successful market timing requires a combination of research, analysis, and a long-term investment perspective. Investors should carefully evaluate local market factors, economic conditions, and their own investment goals to develop a strategic approach to market timing and equity growth. When executed effectively, market timing strategies can significantly enhance the performance of a real estate portfolio and lead to long-term wealth accumulation.

Equity Partnerships

Equity partnerships offer a powerful avenue for real estate investors to pool their resources and participate in larger, more lucrative investments. By partnering with other investors or entities, individuals can access opportunities that may be beyond their individual capacity, whether in terms of capital, expertise, or risk tolerance. Let's delve into the details of equity partnerships and how they enable investors to leverage collective resources for larger investments:

Shared Capital for Larger Deals

One of the primary advantages of equity partnerships is the ability to combine capital from multiple investors to fund larger real estate transactions. This pooling of resources allows investors to participate in acquisitions, developments, or projects that may require substantial funding beyond what any single investor could provide. As a result, investors can access larger and potentially more profitable opportunities that may not be feasible on an individual basis.

Risk Sharing and Diversification

Equity partnerships also facilitate risk sharing among investors. By spreading the financial risk across multiple parties, investors can mitigate their exposure to potential losses. If one property or project underperforms, the impact on each individual investor is reduced compared to bearing the full risk alone. Additionally, equity partnerships enable diversification across multiple properties or projects within a single partnership, further reducing risk.

Access to Expertise and Resources

Partnerships often bring together individuals with diverse skill sets, expertise, and resources. For example, one partner may have experience in property management, while another may excel in financial analysis or market research. By leveraging each partner's strengths, the partnership can benefit from a well-rounded team with the capabilities to effectively manage and optimize the investment. Additionally, partnerships may have access to specialized resources such as legal counsel, property managers, or contractors, enhancing the efficiency and effectiveness of the investment.

Increased Deal Flow and Opportunities

Equity partnerships can also result in increased deal flow and access to a broader range of investment opportunities. As partners share their networks, connections, and market insights, they can uncover off-market deals, exclusive opportunities, or properties with high growth potential. The collective efforts of the partnership enable investors to stay informed about the latest trends, developments, and emerging markets, opening doors to new investment avenues.

Flexibility in Investment Structures

Equity partnerships offer flexibility in structuring deals to suit the preferences and objectives of the partners. Depending on the agreement, partners may have varying levels of involvement, decision-making authority, and profit-sharing arrangements. For example, some partnerships may have active and passive investors, where active partners are involved in day-to-day management, while passive partners provide capital. This flexibility allows partners to tailor the partnership to their individual preferences and roles.

Tax Benefits and Efficiency

Partnerships can also provide tax advantages and efficiencies for investors. Depending on the structure, income and losses from the partnership may flow through to the individual partners, who can then benefit from deductions, depreciation, and other tax benefits associated with real estate investing. Additionally, certain structures, such as Limited Liability Companies (LLCs) or Limited Partnerships (LPs), offer liability protection for partners while providing tax advantages.

Alignment of Interests and Long-Term Vision

Successful equity partnerships are built on alignment of interests and a shared long-term vision. Partnerships typically involve a formal agreement outlining the roles, responsibilities, goals, and exit strategies of each partner. This alignment ensures that all parties are working towards common objectives and are committed to the success of the investment. Clear communication, transparency, and trust among partners are essential for a productive and successful partnership.

In conclusion, equity partnerships offer real estate investors a compelling opportunity to pool their resources, expertise, and networks for larger and more diversified investments. By sharing capital, risks, and responsibilities, investors can access opportunities that may not be feasible individually, while also benefiting from enhanced deal flow, expertise, and tax efficiencies. Successful partnerships are built on collaboration, alignment of interests, and a shared long-term vision for the investment. As real estate markets evolve and opportunities arise, equity partnerships provide a dynamic and effective approach for investors to maximize returns, mitigate risks, and achieve their investment goals.

Real Estate Syndication

Real estate syndication is a specialized form of partnership that allows investors to pool their resources to acquire, develop, or manage real estate properties. This collaborative approach enables individual investors to access larger and more sophisticated real estate opportunities that may otherwise be out of reach. Let's delve into the details of real estate syndication and how it provides investors with access to equity opportunities:

Syndication Structure

In a real estate syndication, a sponsor or lead investor (often a seasoned real estate professional) identifies an investment opportunity and creates a legal entity, such as a Limited Liability Company (LLC) or Limited Partnership (LP), to acquire and manage the property. The sponsor then offers ownership shares or interests in the entity to individual investors, who become limited partners or members of the syndicate.

Access to Larger Properties

One of the primary benefits of real estate syndication is the ability to access larger and more lucrative properties. By pooling together capital from multiple investors, the syndicate has the financial strength to acquire commercial properties, multifamily complexes, or other high-value assets that may require significant funding. This allows individual investors to participate in institutional-grade properties with potential for substantial returns.

Diversification and Risk Mitigation

Real estate syndication also offers investors the benefit of diversification. Instead of putting all their capital into a single property, investors can spread their investment across multiple properties within the syndicate's portfolio. This diversification helps mitigate risk by reducing exposure to the performance of any single asset. Even if one property underperforms, the impact on the overall portfolio is cushioned by the other properties.

Professional Management and Expertise

Syndications are typically led by experienced real estate professionals who serve as the sponsor or general partner. These sponsors bring expertise in property acquisition, management, financing, and market analysis. Their role is to oversee the day-to-day operations of the property, make strategic decisions, and optimize the investment for maximum returns. Investors benefit from the sponsor's knowledge and skills without the need for hands-on involvement in property management.

Passive Investment Opportunity

For passive investors, real estate syndication offers a hands-off investment opportunity. Once they have invested capital into the syndicate, limited partners have little to no involvement in the day-to-day management of the property. This passive approach allows investors to enjoy the benefits of real estate ownership, such as rental income and potential appreciation, without the responsibilities of property maintenance or tenant management.

Tax Advantages

Real estate syndication can also provide tax advantages for investors. Similar to other real estate investments, syndications offer deductions for expenses such as mortgage interest, property taxes, depreciation, and operational costs. Additionally, certain syndication structures, such as a Delaware Statutory Trust (DST) or Tenancy-in-Common (TIC), may offer tax-deferred exchanges and pass-through tax treatment, allowing investors to reduce their taxable income and potentially defer capital gains taxes.

Equity Growth and Cash Flow

Investing in a real estate syndication provides opportunities for both equity growth and cash flow. As the property appreciates in value over time, investors' ownership interests also increase in value. This equity growth can result in substantial returns upon sale or refinancing of the property. Additionally, syndicated properties often generate rental income, which is distributed to investors as regular cash flow distributions.

Investor Protections and Transparency

Real estate syndications are subject to securities regulations and must provide detailed offering documents to investors. These documents outline the terms of the investment, including the property details, financial projections, potential risks, and the rights and responsibilities of investors. This transparency allows investors to make informed decisions and ensures that the syndication complies with legal requirements.

Exit Strategies

Syndications typically have a defined investment horizon and exit strategy. The sponsor may plan to sell the property after a certain period, refinance to extract equity, or execute a 1031 exchange into another property. Investors are typically provided with a clear timeline for the investment, including projected hold period and potential returns. Having a well-defined exit strategy allows investors to plan for the realization of their investment gains.

In conclusion, real estate syndication offers investors a powerful avenue to access equity opportunities in larger, professionally managed properties. By participating in a syndicate, investors can benefit from diversification, professional management, passive investment opportunities, tax advantages, and the potential for equity growth and cash flow. Syndication allows individual investors to leverage their resources and expertise of experienced sponsors to participate in high-value real estate investments that may not be feasible on an individual basis. As with any investment, thorough due diligence and understanding of the syndication terms are essential for making informed decisions. Real estate syndication remains a popular and effective strategy for investors seeking exposure to commercial, multifamily, or other high-value real estate assets.

Equity Exchanges: Swapping for Strategic Growth

Equity exchanges, also known as 1031 exchanges, provide real estate investors with a powerful tool for strategic growth and portfolio expansion. This tax-deferred exchange allows investors to swap one investment property for another of equal or greater value, deferring capital gains taxes that would normally be due upon the sale of the property. Let's delve into the details of equity exchanges and how they can be used for strategic growth:

Tax-Deferred Exchange Basics

A 1031 exchange gets its name from Section 1031 of the Internal Revenue Code, which allows investors to defer capital gains taxes on the sale of investment property if they reinvest the proceeds into a like-kind property. The key requirements of a 1031 exchange include:

- The properties involved must be held for investment or business use, not for personal use.
- The properties must be of like-kind, which generally means they are of the same nature or character, such as real estate for real estate.
- The investor has a specific timeline to identify potential replacement properties (45 days) and complete the exchange (180 days).

Benefits of Equity Exchanges

Tax Deferral: One of the primary benefits of a 1031 exchange is the ability to defer capital gains taxes. When an investor sells a property and reinvests the proceeds into a like-kind property, the capital gains tax liability is deferred until a later date. This allows investors to preserve more of their equity for reinvestment, rather than paying taxes on the sale.

Increased Buying Power: By deferring taxes through a 1031 exchange, investors have more buying power to acquire a higher-value replacement property. Since the full proceeds from the sale are reinvested, including the capital gains that would have been taxed, investors can leverage their equity to acquire a larger, more valuable property. This facilitates strategic growth and portfolio expansion.

Diversification: Equity exchanges also enable investors to diversify their portfolios. Instead of being locked into a single property, investors can exchange into different types of properties, locations, or asset classes. For example, an investor may exchange a single-family rental property for a multifamily apartment complex, diversifying their income streams and spreading risk across multiple properties.

Consolidation or Upgrading: Investors can use 1031 exchanges to consolidate their holdings or upgrade to higher-performing properties. For instance, an investor may exchange multiple smaller properties for a larger, more efficient property with greater income potential. This allows for optimization of the portfolio and enhancement of cash flow and equity growth.

Estate Planning and Wealth Transfer: 1031 exchanges can also be used as part of an estate planning strategy. By deferring taxes through exchanges, investors can continue to grow their real estate portfolios during their lifetime. When the properties are eventually passed on to heirs, the tax basis of the properties is stepped up to their fair market value at the time of inheritance, potentially eliminating the capital gains tax liability altogether.

Timing and Flexibility: Investors have a specific timeline to complete a 1031 exchange, which includes identifying potential replacement properties within 45 days of the sale. This provides some flexibility to search for suitable properties that align with their investment goals. Additionally, investors can execute delayed exchanges, where a qualified intermediary holds the proceeds from the sale until the replacement property is identified and acquired.

Considerations and Requirements

Qualified Intermediary: Investors must use a qualified intermediary (QI) to facilitate the exchange. The QI holds the proceeds from the sale and ensures that the exchange complies with IRS regulations.

Like-Kind Requirement: While like-kind does not mean identical, the properties involved must be of the same nature or character. For example, commercial real estate can be exchanged for residential rental properties.

Timing: Strict timelines must be followed, including the identification of potential replacement properties within 45 days of the sale and completing the exchange within 180 days.

Equal or Greater Value: The replacement property must have a value equal to or greater than the property being sold to fully defer capital gains taxes.

In conclusion, equity exchanges, or 1031 exchanges, offer real estate investors a powerful mechanism for strategic growth, tax deferral, and portfolio optimization. By deferring capital gains taxes, investors can reinvest their equity into larger, more valuable properties, diversify their portfolios, and upgrade or consolidate holdings. 1031 exchanges provide increased buying power, flexibility in investment choices, and opportunities for long-term wealth accumulation. However, these exchanges require careful planning, adherence to IRS regulations, and the use of a qualified intermediary. When used strategically, equity exchanges can be a valuable tool for real estate investors seeking to maximize returns and achieve their investment objectives.

Portfolio Diversification

Portfolio diversification is a fundamental strategy in real estate investing that involves spreading risk across a variety of properties and asset classes. By diversifying their portfolios, investors aim to minimize the impact of any one property's underperformance while maximizing the potential for long-term equity growth. Let's explore the importance of portfolio diversification in real estate:

Risk Mitigation

Diversification is a crucial risk management tool for real estate investors. By spreading investments across different types of properties, locations, and asset classes, investors reduce their exposure to the risks associated with any single property or market. For example, economic downturns or local market fluctuations that affect one property may not have the same impact on others in the portfolio. This risk mitigation strategy helps safeguard against significant losses.

Property Types and Classes

Portfolio diversification can include investing in various types of properties, such as residential, commercial, industrial, retail, or mixed-use properties. Each property type has its own risk and return profile, with some being more sensitive to economic cycles than others. Additionally, investors can diversify within property classes by investing in different quality grades (Class A, B, or C) or property sizes (small multifamily vs. large commercial).

Geographic Diversification

Investors can diversify their portfolios by investing in properties located in different geographic regions. Real estate markets can vary widely based on factors such as job growth, population trends, economic stability, and local demand. Investing in properties in diverse locations helps mitigate the risk of a downturn in any single market. For example, if one region experiences a slowdown, properties in other regions may continue to perform well.

Asset Allocation

Strategic asset allocation involves determining the optimal mix of property types and locations within a portfolio. This includes considering factors such as the investor's risk tolerance, investment goals, market conditions, and economic outlook. A well-balanced portfolio may include a mix of high-risk/high-return properties, stable income-producing assets, and properties with growth potential.

Income vs. Growth Properties

Investors can diversify their portfolios based on the balance between income-producing properties and properties with growth potential. Income properties, such as multifamily apartment buildings or commercial properties with long-term leases, provide steady rental income. On the other hand, growth properties, such as development projects or properties in emerging markets, offer the potential for higher appreciation but may have higher risk.

Asset Class Diversification

Beyond direct property investments, investors can diversify their real estate portfolios by considering other asset classes within the sector. This includes real estate investment trusts (REITs), real estate crowdfunding platforms, mortgage-backed securities, real estate mutual funds, and exchange-traded funds (ETFs). These indirect investments provide exposure to real estate while offering diversification benefits and liquidity.

Risk vs. Return

Portfolio diversification involves balancing risk and return. While diversification can reduce overall portfolio risk, it also impacts potential returns. Generally, higher-risk properties or markets may offer the potential for greater returns but come with increased volatility. Lower-risk properties, such as stabilized income-producing assets, may provide more stable returns but with lower growth potential. Investors must align their diversification strategy with their risk tolerance and investment objectives.

Monitoring and Rebalancing

Maintaining a diversified real estate portfolio requires ongoing monitoring and periodic rebalancing. Market conditions, economic trends, and property performance can change over time. Investors should regularly review their portfolio's composition and make adjustments as needed to ensure it remains aligned with their investment goals and risk tolerance. Rebalancing may involve selling over performing assets, acquiring new properties, or adjusting asset allocations.

In conclusion, portfolio diversification is a cornerstone of successful real estate investing. By spreading risk across different properties, property types, locations, and asset classes, investors can minimize the impact of market fluctuations and enhance long-term equity growth. Diversification provides protection against individual property risks while optimizing the potential for overall portfolio performance. Real estate investors should carefully consider their risk tolerance, investment goals, and market conditions when implementing a diversified portfolio strategy. Through strategic asset allocation, geographic diversification, and a mix of income and growth properties, investors can build resilient portfolios that withstand market challenges and capitalize on opportunities for wealth accumulation in the dynamic real estate market.

Commercial Real Estate

Commercial real estate presents unique opportunities for investors to unlock greater equity potential compared to residential properties. Commercial properties, such as office buildings, retail centers, industrial facilities, and multifamily complexes, offer various avenues for increasing equity through appreciation, income generation, and value-added strategies. Let's explore how commercial real estate can be a valuable asset class for investors seeking to grow their equity:

Appreciation Potential

Commercial properties often have greater appreciation potential compared to residential properties. Factors such as location, demand from tenants, economic growth in the area, and improvements to the property can contribute to value appreciation. Well-located commercial properties in thriving markets tend to appreciate in value over time, providing investors with equity growth.

Income Generation

One of the primary ways commercial real estate builds equity is through rental income. Commercial leases are typically longer-term and can include annual rent escalations, providing a steady stream of income for investors. Lease terms for commercial properties are often triple net (NNN), where tenants are responsible for property expenses such as taxes, insurance, and maintenance. This stable income stream contributes to equity growth over time.

Value-Add Opportunities

Commercial real estate offers numerous value-add opportunities for investors to increase equity. Value-add strategies include renovating or repositioning a property to improve its appeal and rental income potential. For example, upgrading common areas, adding amenities, or modernizing building systems can attract higher-quality tenants willing to pay higher rents. Value-add projects can significantly boost a property's value and equity.

Leverage and Financing

Commercial real estate investors can leverage their investments to increase equity growth. Lenders often provide financing for commercial properties, allowing investors to purchase properties with a smaller upfront investment. By using leverage, investors amplify their equity returns. However, it's crucial to manage leverage responsibly to avoid over-leveraging and potential risks.

Tenant Quality and Stability

The quality of commercial tenants can impact equity growth. Properties with high-quality, creditworthy tenants on long-term leases provide stability and predictability in rental income. Lease terms in commercial real estate are typically longer than residential leases, reducing turnover and vacancy risks. Strong tenant covenants can enhance property value and, consequently, equity.

Market Demand and Trends

Understanding market demand and trends is essential for unlocking equity potential in commercial real estate. Investors should assess market fundamentals such as population growth, job creation, infrastructure development, and industry trends. Investing in markets with growing demand for commercial space, such as technology hubs or urban centers undergoing revitalization, can lead to higher property values and equity growth.

Sector and Property Type Selection

Different commercial property sectors offer varying equity growth potential. For example:

Office Buildings: Demand for modern, well-located office spaces can drive appreciation and rental income growth.

Retail Centers: Retail properties with high foot traffic and anchor tenants can be valuable assets, especially in thriving retail corridors.

Industrial Facilities: With the rise of e-commerce and logistics, industrial properties such as warehouses and distribution centers are in high demand, offering strong appreciation potential.

Multifamily Complexes: Apartment buildings and multifamily properties provide steady cash flow and appreciation potential, particularly in rental markets with high demand.

Risk Management and Due Diligence

As with any investment, commercial real estate comes with risks, and investors should conduct thorough due diligence. This includes property inspections, financial analysis, market research, tenant analysis, and understanding lease terms. Risk management strategies such as property insurance, tenant diversification, and proper property management are crucial for protecting and growing equity.

Exit Strategies

Investors should also consider their exit strategies to realize equity gains. Common exit strategies in commercial real estate include:

Sale: Selling the property after it has appreciated in value, potentially realizing substantial equity gains.

Refinancing: Extracting equity by refinancing the property at a higher value, allowing investors to access cash while maintaining ownership.

1031 Exchange: Using a 1031 exchange to defer capital gains taxes and reinvest proceeds into another property, allowing for continued equity growth.

In conclusion, commercial real estate offers investors a pathway to unlock greater equity potential through appreciation, income generation, value-add strategies, and market trends. By investing in well-located properties with strong tenant covenants and growth prospects, investors can build equity over time. Leveraging financing, understanding market demand, selecting the right property types, and implementing effective risk management are key components of successful equity growth in commercial real estate. Investors should align their investment strategies with their risk tolerance, goals, and market conditions to capitalize on the opportunities that commercial real estate presents for long-term wealth accumulation.

Retirement Planning with Real Estate Equity

Retirement planning with real estate equity offers a compelling strategy for building a secure and sustainable financial future. Real estate can serve as a valuable asset class in retirement portfolios, providing income, appreciation, tax advantages, and a hedge against inflation. Let's explore how investors can utilize real estate equity to create a solid foundation for retirement:

Steady Income Stream

One of the primary benefits of real estate for retirement planning is the potential for a steady income stream. Rental properties, such as residential apartments or commercial spaces, can generate reliable rental income month after month. This income can supplement other retirement income sources, such as pensions, Social Security, or retirement accounts. Having a diversified income stream from real estate can provide stability and security during retirement years.

Mortgage Paydown and Equity Growth

Over time, real estate properties also build equity through mortgage paydown and appreciation. As tenants pay rent, part of that income goes towards paying off the property's mortgage. This process of mortgage amortization gradually increases the property owner's equity in the asset. Additionally, real estate historically appreciates over the long term, further boosting equity. This growing equity serves as a valuable nest egg for retirement, allowing investors to tap into it when needed or pass it on to heirs.

Inflation Hedge

Real estate is often considered an effective hedge against inflation. Inflation erodes the purchasing power of money over time, but real estate tends to appreciate in value as prices rise. Rental income also tends to increase with inflation, as landlords can adjust rental rates to keep pace with rising costs. By holding real estate assets, retirees can protect their purchasing power and maintain a reliable income stream that adjusts for inflation.

Tax Advantages

Real estate investments offer various tax advantages that can enhance retirement planning. Rental income from real estate is typically taxed at lower rates than ordinary income. Additionally, investors can deduct expenses such as property taxes, mortgage interest, maintenance costs, and depreciation. Depreciation is a particularly valuable tax benefit that allows investors to deduct a portion of the property's value each year, reducing taxable income. These tax advantages can significantly boost after-tax returns and cash flow for retirees.

Equity Release Options

Retirees can access the equity in their real estate holdings through various means:

Reverse Mortgages: A reverse mortgage allows homeowners aged 62 or older to convert part of their home equity into cash without selling the property. This can provide additional income during retirement, with the loan balance due when the homeowner moves out or passes away.

Cash-Out Refinancing: Retirees can refinance their mortgage to access equity in the property. By refinancing to a new loan with a higher balance, they receive the difference in cash. This option can provide a lump sum of cash for large expenses or investments.

Sell and Downsize: Another option is to sell the property and downsize to a smaller, more manageable home. This can free up equity for retirement expenses while reducing ongoing maintenance and costs associated with a larger property.

Portfolio Diversification

Real estate adds diversification to a retirement portfolio, reducing overall risk. Real estate investments have a low correlation with traditional asset classes like stocks and bonds, meaning they often perform differently in various market conditions. During economic downturns, when stocks may decline, real estate values and rental income can remain stable or even increase. This diversification helps protect retirement savings from market volatility.

Passive Investment and Management

Real estate investments can be passive, providing a source of income without the need for active management. Retirees can hire property managers to handle day-to-day operations, tenant relations, and property maintenance. This passive income stream allows retirees to enjoy a hands-off approach to investing while still benefiting from rental income and equity growth.

Long-Term Growth and Legacy Planning

Real estate investments offer the potential for long-term growth, which is especially valuable for retirement planning. Over time, properties can appreciate significantly, building substantial equity. This equity can be used to fund retirement expenses, support lifestyle choices, or leave a legacy for future generations. Real estate holdings can be passed on to heirs, providing a lasting financial foundation for the family.

In conclusion, retirement planning with real estate equity offers a comprehensive approach to building a secure and comfortable future. Through rental income, mortgage paydown, tax advantages, and inflation protection, real estate can serve as a reliable income source during retirement. Retirees can access equity through various means, such as reverse mortgages or cash-out refinancing, to meet financial needs or enhance lifestyle. Real estate also adds diversification to retirement portfolios, reducing risk and volatility. With its potential for long-term growth and legacy planning, real estate equity plays a vital role in creating a sustainable retirement strategy. By incorporating real estate into retirement planning, individuals can secure their financial well-being and enjoy a fulfilling retirement lifestyle.

Equity Preservation: Protecting Your Real Estate Wealth

Equity preservation is a critical aspect of real estate investing, focusing on strategies and practices to safeguard and protect the value of real estate assets. Preservation of equity involves mitigating risks, maintaining property value, minimizing expenses, and ensuring long-term profitability. Let's delve into the key considerations and strategies for protecting your real estate wealth:

Risk Management

Insurance Coverage: Comprehensive insurance coverage is essential to protect real estate assets from unforeseen events such as natural disasters, fire, theft, liability claims, and other hazards. Property owners should regularly review and update their insurance policies to ensure adequate coverage. This includes property insurance, liability insurance, and umbrella policies to provide additional protection.

Asset Protection Structures: Investors may consider using legal structures such as Limited Liability Companies (LLCs) or Limited Partnerships (LPs) to protect personal assets from potential lawsuits or claims related to the property. These entities can shield personal wealth from liabilities associated with the property, providing an added layer of protection.

Property Maintenance and Upkeep

Regular Inspections and Maintenance: Routine inspections and proactive maintenance are key to preserving property value. Regular inspections allow owners to identify and address issues early, preventing small problems from becoming costly repairs. This includes maintaining HVAC systems, plumbing, roofing, and structural components. Well-maintained properties retain their value and appeal to tenants and buyers.

Tenant Management: For rental properties, effective tenant management is crucial. Screening tenants thoroughly can help reduce the risk of late payments, property damage, or eviction costs. Clear lease agreements outlining tenant responsibilities and property rules can also protect the property and preserve its condition.

Financial Management

Cash Flow Management: Maintaining positive cash flow is vital for preserving equity. Property owners should closely monitor income and expenses, ensuring that rental income covers mortgage payments, property taxes, insurance, maintenance costs, and vacancies. Building a cash reserve for unexpected expenses or vacancies helps avoid financial strain and protects equity.

Debt Management: Careful management of debt is essential to preserve equity. Investors should consider refinancing options to lower interest rates, extend loan terms, or access equity for improvements. Avoiding excessive leverage and maintaining a healthy debt-to-equity ratio reduces financial risk and protects equity in the property.

Market Awareness and Adaptation

Stay Informed: Real estate markets are dynamic and subject to changes in economic conditions, supply and demand, and local trends. Property owners should stay informed about market conditions, rental trends, and property values in their area. This awareness helps in making informed decisions about when to buy, sell, or hold onto properties.

Adaptation to Market Changes: Flexibility and adaptability are crucial for equity preservation. In response to market changes, property owners may need to adjust rental rates, update property amenities, or target new tenant demographics. Being proactive and responsive to market shifts helps maintain property value and rental income.

Legal and Tax Strategies

Legal Compliance: Ensuring compliance with local, state, and federal regulations is essential for equity preservation. Property owners should stay up-to-date with landlord-tenant laws, building codes, zoning regulations, and safety requirements. Non-compliance can lead to fines, penalties, or legal disputes that can erode equity.

Tax Efficiency: Implementing tax-efficient strategies can help preserve equity by minimizing tax liabilities. This includes taking advantage of tax deductions for property expenses, depreciation benefits, and 1031 exchanges for deferring capital gains taxes. Consulting with tax professionals can help optimize tax strategies while protecting equity.

Portfolio Diversification

Spread Risk: Diversifying the real estate portfolio across different property types, locations, and markets spreads risk and protects against localized economic downturns. A diverse portfolio can include residential, commercial, multifamily, and other property types to balance income streams and preserve equity in varying market conditions.

In conclusion, equity preservation is a comprehensive approach to protecting and maintaining the value of real estate investments. Through risk management, property maintenance, financial discipline, market awareness, legal compliance, tax efficiency, and portfolio diversification, investors can safeguard their real estate wealth. By implementing proactive strategies and staying informed about market trends and regulatory changes, property owners can mitigate risks, reduce expenses, and maximize long-term profitability. Equity preservation is not only about protecting current wealth but also ensuring a solid foundation for future growth and financial security. Real estate investors who prioritize equity preservation are better positioned to weather market fluctuations and capitalize on opportunities while maintaining the value of their real estate assets.

Real Estate Exit Strategies

Real estate exit strategies are crucial for investors looking to capitalize on their equity and realize profits from their property investments. These strategies involve carefully planning and executing the sale or disposition of real estate assets to maximize returns. Whether aiming to cash out, reinvest, or transition to other investments, having a well-thought-out exit plan is essential. Let's explore various real estate exit strategies that allow investors to capitalize on their equity for profits:

Sale to Cash Out

Traditional Sale: The most straightforward exit strategy is selling the property on the open market. By listing the property with a real estate agent or broker, investors can attract potential buyers and negotiate a sale price. This strategy allows investors to cash out their equity, receive proceeds from the sale, and potentially realize capital gains.

Auction: An auction can be an effective method for selling real estate quickly and at a competitive price. Auctions create a sense of urgency among buyers, leading to potential bidding wars. This strategy can result in a fast sale and favorable sale price, allowing investors to capitalize on their equity.

Refinancing for Equity Extraction

Cash-Out Refinance: Investors can refinance their property with a new loan that has a higher balance than the existing mortgage. The difference between the new loan amount and the existing mortgage is cashed out, providing investors with access to their equity. This strategy allows investors to retain ownership of the property while accessing funds for other investments or expenses.

1031 Exchange for Tax-Deferred Growth

A 1031 exchange allows investors to defer capital gains taxes by reinvesting proceeds from the sale of one property into a like-kind replacement property. This strategy is beneficial for investors looking to preserve their equity and leverage it to acquire a larger or more lucrative property. By deferring taxes, investors can maximize their investment capital and continue to grow their real estate portfolio.

Lease Option or Rent-to-Own

Lease Option: Investors can offer a lease option to tenants, giving them the right to purchase the property at a specified price within a set period. This strategy allows investors to generate rental income while giving tenants the opportunity to buy the property. If the tenant exercises the option to purchase, investors can capitalize on their equity by selling the property at the agreed-upon price.

Value-Add and Improve

Renovation and Repositioning: Investors can increase the property's value through strategic renovations and improvements. By enhancing the property's appeal, functionality, or amenities, investors can attract higher-quality tenants willing to pay higher rents. This value-add strategy can significantly boost the property's market value and equity.

Joint Ventures or Partnerships

Equity Partnership Sale: Investors can sell their equity stake in a property to a partner or joint venture. This strategy allows investors to exit the investment while realizing profits from their equity share. Joint ventures or partnerships can be structured to provide liquidity to investors while allowing the property to continue operating under new ownership.

Owner Financing or Seller Financing

Seller Financing: Investors can offer seller financing to potential buyers, acting as the lender for the property sale. This strategy allows investors to sell the property while receiving regular mortgage payments from the buyer. Seller financing can attract more buyers, especially those who may not qualify for traditional financing, and provide investors with ongoing income.

Sell Partial Ownership or Equity

Investors can sell a partial ownership stake or equity share in the property to another investor. This strategy allows investors to cash out a portion of their equity while retaining ownership of the property. Selling partial ownership can provide liquidity and diversify investment holdings.

In conclusion, real estate exit strategies offer investors various options to capitalize on their equity for profits. Whether aiming to cash out, reinvest, defer taxes, or transition to other investments, selecting the right exit strategy depends on factors such as market conditions, investment goals, tax implications, and the property's condition. By carefully planning and executing an exit strategy, investors can maximize their returns, realize profits from their real estate investments, and strategically manage their portfolios. It's essential for investors to evaluate each exit strategy's benefits and risks, consult with real estate professionals, and align their strategy with their overall financial objectives. Real estate exit strategies provide flexibility and opportunities for investors to leverage their equity for long-term wealth creation and financial success.

The Future of Real Estate Equity

The future of real estate equity is shaped by evolving trends, technological advancements, and innovative strategies that are poised to drive continued growth and transformation in the industry. As we look ahead, several key trends and innovations are likely to impact the real estate market and how investors approach equity accumulation. Let's explore these trends and their implications for the future of real estate equity:

Technology Integration

PropTech Solutions: The integration of technology into real estate, known as PropTech, is revolutionizing the industry. Innovations such as virtual reality (VR) property tours, 3D modeling, and augmented reality (AR) applications are enhancing the property viewing experience for buyers and tenants. These technologies allow investors to showcase properties remotely, attracting a broader audience and increasing property visibility.

Smart Buildings and IoT: Smart buildings equipped with Internet of Things (IoT) devices are becoming increasingly prevalent. These connected buildings feature sensors, smart thermostats, security systems, and energy management tools. Investors can leverage IoT technology to improve operational efficiency, reduce maintenance costs, and enhance tenant experiences. Smart buildings can command higher rents and property values, leading to increased equity growth.

Sustainability and Green Buildings

ESG Investing: Environmental, Social, and Governance (ESG) considerations are gaining prominence in real estate investment decisions. Investors are increasingly focused on sustainability, energy efficiency, and green building certifications such as LEED (Leadership in Energy and Environmental Design). Properties with ESG features are attractive to environmentally conscious tenants and investors, leading to higher occupancy rates and property values.

Net-Zero Buildings: The trend towards net-zero energy buildings, which produce as much energy as they consume, is gaining momentum. Investors in net-zero buildings benefit from reduced operating costs, increased asset value, and a competitive edge in the market. These sustainable properties are likely to command premium rents and attract socially responsible investors, contributing to equity growth.

Co-Living and Co-Working Spaces

Shared Spaces: The rise of co-living and co-working spaces is reshaping the real estate landscape. Co-living developments offer shared living spaces and amenities, appealing to young professionals and digital nomads seeking community-oriented living arrangements. Co-working spaces provide flexible work environments for startups, freelancers, and remote workers. Investors can capitalize on this trend by investing in mixed-use developments that combine residential, office, and communal spaces, driving equity growth through diverse income streams.

Demographic Shifts and Urbanization

Aging Population: The aging population is creating demand for senior living communities and healthcare facilities. Investors can target these sectors to capitalize on the growing need for specialized housing and healthcare services. Properties designed for active senior living, assisted living, and memory care facilities present opportunities for equity growth as the demographic landscape evolves.

Urban Revitalization: Urbanization continues to drive demand for urban living spaces, particularly among younger generations. Investors can focus on urban redevelopment projects, mixed-use developments, and transit-oriented properties in vibrant city centers. These properties benefit from proximity to amenities, public transportation, and cultural attractions, attracting tenants and driving property values.

Alternative Investment Models

Real Estate Crowdfunding: Crowdfunding platforms offer investors new avenues to access real estate investments. Through real estate crowdfunding, investors can participate in projects with lower capital requirements, diversify their portfolios, and access a broader range of properties. This democratization of real estate investing opens opportunities for investors to build equity across multiple projects and asset classes.

Tokenization and Blockchain: Blockchain technology enables the tokenization of real estate assets, allowing investors to purchase fractional ownership through digital tokens. Tokenization provides liquidity, transparency, and accessibility to real estate markets. Investors can trade tokens on digital platforms, unlocking liquidity and creating a more liquid market for real estate equity.

In conclusion, the future of real estate equity is characterized by technological advancements, sustainability, changing demographics, and innovative investment models. Investors can position themselves for continued growth by embracing these trends and strategies:

Technology Integration

Sustainability: Investing in green buildings, net-zero energy properties, and ESG-focused assets for higher occupancy and property values.

Co-Living and Co-Working: Targeting shared living and working spaces to cater to evolving lifestyle preferences and work trends.

Demographic Shifts: Capitalizing on the aging population with senior living and healthcare investments, and urbanization trends with urban redevelopment projects.

Alternative Investment Models: Exploring real estate crowdfunding, tokenization, and blockchain for diversified and accessible investment opportunities.

By staying informed about these trends, adopting innovative technologies, and embracing sustainable and socially responsible practices, real estate investors can navigate the evolving landscape and continue to grow their equity in the dynamic real estate market of the future. The future of real estate equity is shaped by these trends and innovations, offering exciting opportunities for investors to build wealth, drive sustainability, and create value in their real estate portfolios.

Final thought

In conclusion, "Building Equity: Proven Techniques for Growing Your Real Estate Portfolio" offers a comprehensive roadmap for real estate investors aiming to maximize equity growth and build lasting wealth. Throughout this book, we have explored the multifaceted world of real estate equity, from its foundational principles to advanced strategies and emerging trends. Here are the key takeaways that investors can apply to their journey toward financial success:

Real estate equity is a powerful wealth-building tool, offering the potential for appreciation, rental income, tax advantages, and portfolio diversification. Understanding the foundations of equity is the cornerstone of successful real estate investing, providing investors with the knowledge to make informed decisions and capitalize on opportunities.

Strategic property selection is a critical aspect of building a successful real estate portfolio. By carefully considering factors such as location, market demand, property types, and growth potential, investors can lay a solid foundation for equity growth. The right property selection sets the stage for long-term profitability and wealth accumulation.

Leveraging leverage intelligently can amplify equity growth. Using financing strategically to acquire properties, fund renovations, or unlock equity can accelerate wealth accumulation. However, investors must exercise caution and prudence to manage leverage responsibly and avoid overexposure to risk.

Equity through renovations and value-add strategies offers investors a pathway to increase property value and enhance equity. Upgrading properties, improving amenities, and focusing on energy efficiency can attract higher-quality tenants and command higher rents, ultimately boosting equity growth.

Long-term buy-and-hold strategies are fundamental for building a secure real estate portfolio. Patiently holding onto properties allows investors to benefit from appreciation, rental income, and equity accumulation over time. This strategy is particularly effective for those seeking stable, long-term growth in their equity.

Innovative equity strategies, such as equity crowdfunding, real estate syndication, and blockchain tokenization, provide investors with diverse options to access real estate opportunities and grow their equity. These emerging approaches open up new avenues for investors to participate in real estate projects and diversify their portfolios.

Tax-efficient strategies and equity preservation are crucial for long-term wealth preservation. Maximizing returns through tax planning, risk management, and proper property maintenance ensures that investors can protect and grow their equity over time. Understanding the tax implications of real estate investments is essential for optimizing returns and preserving wealth.

As we look to the future of real estate equity, technological advancements, sustainability, demographic shifts, and alternative investment models will continue to shape the landscape. Investors who stay informed, adapt to emerging trends, and embrace innovation will be well-positioned to capitalize on opportunities for growth and continued success in the dynamic real estate market.

"Building Equity" serves as a comprehensive guide for investors at all levels, providing actionable insights, proven techniques, and strategic approaches for navigating the complexities of real estate investing. Whether you are a novice investor looking to build your first portfolio or an experienced professional seeking to optimize equity growth, this book offers a roadmap for success.

By implementing the principles outlined in "Building Equity," investors can navigate the real estate market with confidence, make informed decisions, and build a robust and profitable portfolio over time. Real estate equity is a powerful vehicle for wealth creation, and with the right strategies and mindset, investors can achieve their financial goals and secure a prosperous future.

www.ingramcontent.com/pod-product-compliance
Lightning Source LLC
Chambersburg PA
CBHW050107230526
45470CB00004B/1719